KB244199

A Day in Space

Happy House

About Wise & Wide

- A systematic 6-level English reading program based on Lexile® measures
- Diverse and interesting topics chosen from the elementary curriculums of Korea and English speaking western countries
- Well-written books in various forms including fiction stories, descriptive texts, and classics retold
- The informative but original fiction stories grab your interest, leading to the easy and clear understanding of the educational content.
- Improve thinking skills with solid after-reading activities at all levels of the series.

Wise & Wide is a 6-level English reading program that consists of 60 books and each level is systematically divided by Lexile® measures. The Lexile® Framework for Reading is the most popular reading measuring system in American formal education curriculums and many English programs. Over 20 out of 50 states in the U.S. mark Lexile® measures directly on students' final report cards and over 300 well-known publishers adopt and use Lexile® measures.

Experience many kinds of readings written by professional writers from the U.S. and England. They used interesting topics that were carefully chosen after analyzing elementary curriculums from around the world including Korea, the U.S., England, and Australia among many others. Comprehensive after-reading activities including graphic organizers, speaking tasks, and After-reading Tests are ready for you.

Levels in the series and their corresponding Lexile® measures

Level	Lexile® measures	U.S. Grade
Level 1	Below 200L	Pre K - K
Level 2	190L - 400L	Lower Grade 1
Level 3	350L - 530L	Upper Grade 1
Level 4	420L - 650L	Grade 2
Level 5	520L - 940L	Grade 3 - 4
Level 6	830L - 1070L	Grade 5 - 6

* Smart Readers: Wise & Wide level 1 is applicable to the preschool level in the U.S.
* The source of the relationship between Lexile® measures and U.S. school grades: CCSS(Common Core State Standards) FOR ENGLISH LANGUAGE ARTS, APPENDIX A (2012, which is used by 45 states in the U.S.)

Topic List

	Level 1	Level 2	Level 3	Level 4	Level 5	Level 6
Book 1	Science>Biology: The hibernation of animals Story	Science>Biology: Living and nonliving things Story	Science>Biology> Animals & the Environment: Sea otters Story	Environment> Living with nature: The diver & the persimmon tree Story	Science>Biology> Animal: Amazing animals of the Amazon Story	Science>Biology: Germs, transmitted diseases Story
Book 2	Literature> World classics: Aesop's fables Story	Literature> Traditional fairy tale: Old tales about stones Story	Social Studies> Economy: To run a business to make and save money Story	Science>Biology> Plants: Photosynthesis Story	Science>Earth science: Earth's layers, earthquakes, volcanoes, and earth's atmosphere Report	Mathematics> Sequence: The golden ratio & the Fibonacci sequence Story
Book 3	Science>Physics: How shadows are formed Story	Literature> World classics: Peter Pan Story	Science>Scientific technology: Nanobots Story	Literature>Myths: World's creation stories Story	Literature> Legend: The story of King Arthur Story	Literature>Myths: Constellation myths Story
Book 4	Literature> Traditional literature: The Talmud Story	Science>Biology> Animal: Polar bears Story	Science>Biology> Animal: Mountain gorillas Story	Social Studies> Cultural anthropology: Amazing ancient cultures of the world Story	Science> Earth science: Clouds and weather Story	Literature> Human & animals: The friendship between a girl and a horse Story
Book 5	Social Studies> Ethics: Rules in daily life Story	Science>Biology: The five senses Report	Social Studies> Cultural anthropology: Astonishing festivals Report	Art>Music: Stories from two operas Story	Social Studies> World culture & history: The Renaissance Story	Sports> Board sports: Surfing & snowboarding Story
Book 6	Social Studies> World geography & travel: Tourist attractions around the world Story	Science>Biology> Animal: Dinosaurs Story	Science> Astronomy: The solar system Story	Social Studies> People: Three great people who overcame hardships Story	Science>Scientific technology: The wonderful world of robots Report	Art>Music: Composers of the Romantic Era Report
Book 7	Science> Space science: The life of astronauts Report	Social Studies> Cultural anthropology: Mythological monsters from around the world Report	Mathematics> Elementary mathematics: Numbers, measurement, shapes and data Report	Science & Social Studies> Technology & culture: Inventions from around the world Report	Art>Works of art: Famous paintings Report	Social Studies> Human & animals: Animals in action for human Report
Book 8	Social Studies> Cultural anthropology: Various living cultures of the world Story	Art>Music: Instruments in the orchestra Story	Social Studies> Life safety: Learning and using outdoor survival skills Story	Social Studies> History: The California Gold Rush Report	Social Studies & Science> Psychology: Psychology in everyday life Story	Literature> World classics: The Merchant of Venice Story
Book 9	Social Studies> Jobs: Interviews about jobs Report	Science>Scientific technology: Developments in technology in different times Story	Social Studies> Politics>Election: Running for 3rd grade class president Story	Literature> World classics: Stories of Sherlock Holmes Story	Literature> World classics: Adrift in the Pacific Story	
Book 10		Sports>Winter sports: Various aspects of some Winter Olympic sports Report				

* 10 books in each level will be published.

How to Use This Book

•Before Reading

You can easily find the topic and what kind of story you are about to read.

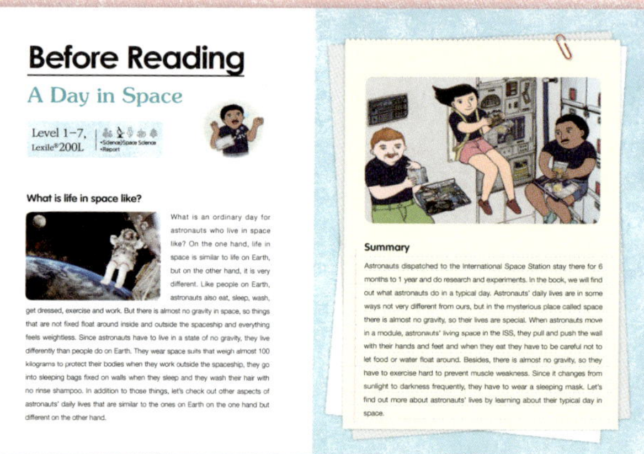

•The text

All the stories were written by professional writers from the U.S. and England, so you will read authentic and appropriate English sentences and expressions in every book in the series.

•Pop Quiz

Check out right away if you understand what you have just read by solving a pop quiz that checks your comprehension.

•Key Words

The key words and expressions on each page are listed for you to easily study them.

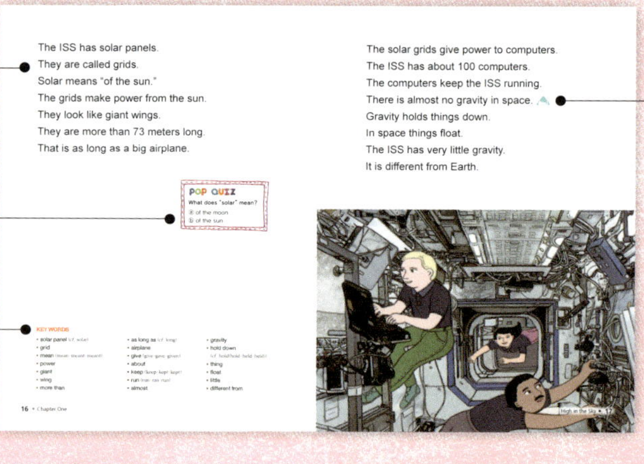

•Aha! Tips

Download free Korean explanations at *www.ihappyhouse.co.kr* for all of the sentences marked with "Aha!". These explain cultural, scientific, and economic knowledge or they deal with aspects of English such as grammatical structures or idiomatic expressions. There are lots of "Aha! Tips" to help you understand the text.

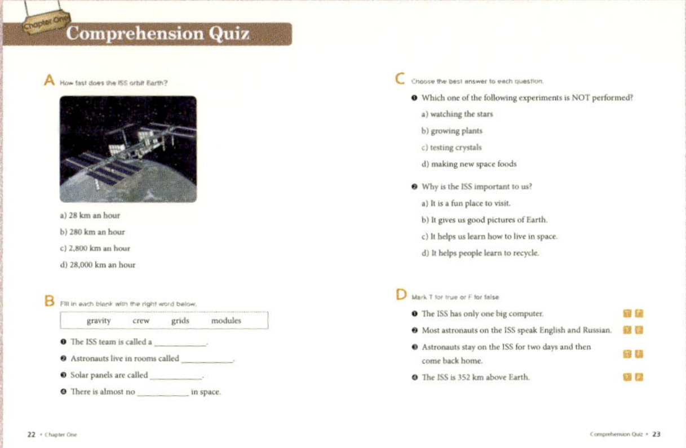

•Comprehension Quiz

After reading one chapter, solve various questions to find out if you fully understand the content.

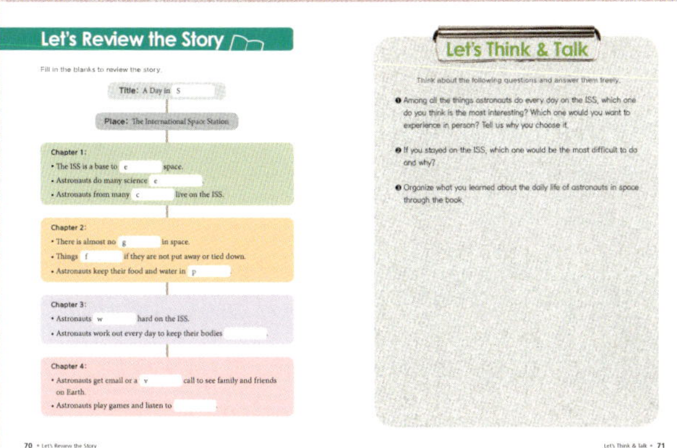

•Let's Review the Story /
•Let's Think & Talk

Fill in the blanks in the organizer to summarize the whole story. Express your own thinking and feelings about the story by answering the questions. You can build up logic and reasoning skills for your essay examinations in the future.

Appendix

Audio CD

In the CD audio book form, the texts are read vividly by American professional voice actors. (MP3 files downloaded for free)

After-reading Test

Solve an additionally provided After-reading Test for each book.

The Korean translation, Answer Keys, a Word Quiz, a Word List, and Aha! Tips for each book

You can download them for free at *www.ihappyhouse.co.kr* or *www.darakwon.co.kr*

Before Reading

A Day in Space

What is life in space like?

What is an ordinary day for astronauts who live in space like? On the one hand, life in space is similar to life on Earth, but on the other hand, it is very different. Like people on Earth, astronauts also eat, sleep, wash, get dressed, exercise and work. But there is almost no gravity in space, so things that are not fixed float around inside and outside the spaceship and everything feels weightless. Since astronauts have to live in a state of no gravity, they live differently than people do on Earth. They wear space suits that weigh almost 100 kilograms to protect their bodies when they work outside the spaceship, they go into sleeping bags fixed on walls when they sleep and they wash their hair with no rinse shampoo. In addition to those things, let's check out other aspects of astronauts' daily lives that are similar to the ones on Earth on the one hand but different on the other hand.

Summary

Astronauts dispatched to the International Space Station stay there for 6 months to 1 year and do research and experiments. In the book, we will find out what astronauts do in a typical day. Astronauts' daily lives are in some ways not very different from ours, but in the mysterious place called space there is almost no gravity, so their lives are special. When astronauts move in a module, astronauts' living space in the ISS, they pull and push the wall with their hands and feet and when they eat they have to be careful not to let food or water float around. Besides, there is almost no gravity, so they have to exercise hard to prevent muscle weakness. Since it changes from sunlight to darkness frequently, they have to wear a sleeping mask. Let's find out more about astronauts' lives by learning about their typical day in space.

Contents

A Day in Space

A Day in Space

High in the Sky

Look up at the sky.

Look high above Earth.

There is a place in space.

It is the International Space Station. 

It is called the ISS.

At night, you can see it fly by.

It looks like a moving star.

The ISS is a place to live.

It is a place to work.

It is a base to explore space.

KEY WORDS

- high
- look up
- high above
- earth
- place
- space

- International Space Station(ISS)
- **be called** (*cf.* call)
- can + *Verb*
- **see** (see-saw-seen)
- **fly by** (fly-flew-flown)
- look like

- **moving** (*cf.* move)
- star
- live
- work
- base
- explore

Astronauts live there.

They are from many different countries.

The ISS flies around Earth.

It flies in an orbit.

It is 352 kilometers high.

It goes 28,000 kilometers an hour!

That is fast!

It orbits Earth in 92 minutes!

The ISS is big.

It is over 100 meters wide.

That is longer than a football field.

Astronauts live on the ISS.

They work in space.

Some live there six months.

Some live there a year.

Some live there longer.

They live in rooms called modules.

They work in these rooms too.

The modules are like tubes.

Each one has a name.

One has a dome.

The dome has many windows.

The astronauts look out the windows.

They look at Earth.

- like
- tube
- each
- name
- one
- dome
- window
- look out
- look at

They take pictures of Earth.

They are high in the sky.

The astronauts take videos.

They record sunrises.

They record sunsets.

KEY WORDS

- take a picture of (take-took-taken)
- take a video
- record
- sunrise
- sunset

The ISS has solar panels.

They are called grids.

Solar means "of the sun."

The grids make power from the sun.

They look like giant wings.

They are more than 73 meters long.

That is as long as a big airplane.

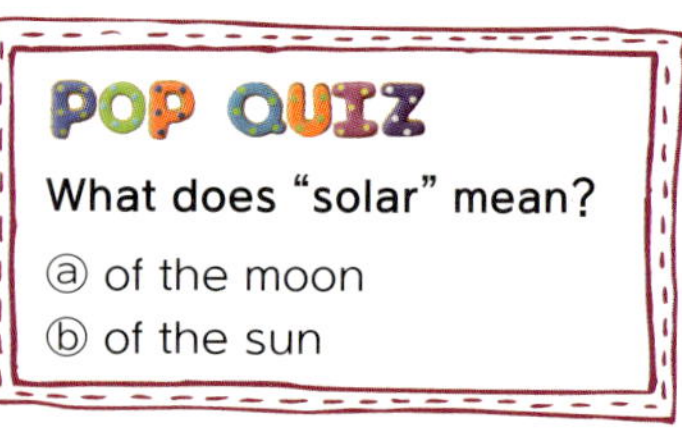

KEY WORDS

- **solar panel** (*cf.* solar)
- **grid**
- **mean** (mean-meant-meant)
- **power**
- **giant**
- **wing**
- **more than**

- **as long as** (*cf.* long)
- **airplane**
- **give** (give-gave-given)
- **about**
- **keep** (keep-kept-kept)
- **run** (run-ran-run)
- **almost**

- **gravity**
- **hold down** (hold-held-held)
- **thing**
- **float**
- **little**
- **different from**

The solar grids give power to computers.

The ISS has about 100 computers.

The computers keep the ISS running.

There is almost no gravity in space. 

Gravity holds things down.

In space things float.

The ISS has very little gravity.

It is different from Earth.

Astronauts do science experiments in space.

They want to see how things work in space.

Astronauts work on many things.

There are more than 200 experiments! **Aha!**

One is watching the stars.

Another is growing plants.

One is testing crystals.

Another is working with a robot.

There are so many things to learn in space.

We can learn from the ISS.

The astronauts study many things.

The astronauts tell us what they learn.

We can learn about medicine.

We can learn about our bodies.

We can learn about plants.

The ISS helps us learn how to get along.

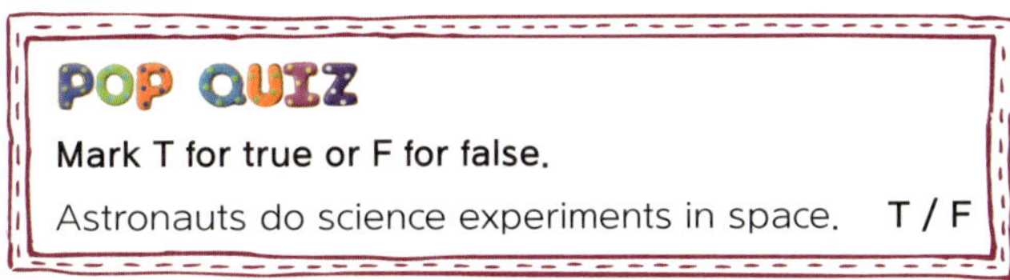

KEY WORDS

- **do** (do-did-done)
- science
- experiment
- want
- how
- on
- watch

- another
- **grow** (grow-grew-grown)
- plant
- test
- crystal
- robot
- learn

- study
- **tell** (tell-told-told)
- medicine
- body
- help
- how to + *Verb*
- **get along** (get-got-gotten)

The ISS has two captains.

One is Russian.

The other is American.

Astronauts on the ISS speak many languages.

Most speak English and Russian.

Everyone works as a team.

The team is called a crew.

- captain
- Russian
- the other
- American

- speak
  (speak-spoke-spoken)
- language
- most

- everyone
- as
- team
- crew

Up to six people live in the ISS.

Some of the crew are men.

Some of the crew are women.

Someday people may go to Mars.

Someday people may live on the moon.

Astronauts are learning how to live in space.

This will help us live in space someday.

KEY WORDS

- up to
- people
- men (*cf.* women)
- someday
- may + *Verb*
- Mars
- moon
- will + *Verb*

Chapter One

Comprehension Quiz

A How fast does the ISS orbit Earth?

a) 28 km an hour

b) 280 km an hour

c) 2,800 km an hour

d) 28,000 km an hour

B Fill in each blank with the right word below.

gravity	crew	grids	modules

❶ The ISS team is called a ______________.

❷ Astronauts live in rooms called ______________.

❸ Solar panels are called ______________.

❹ There is almost no ______________ in space.

C Choose the best answer to each question.

❶ Which one of the following experiments is NOT performed?

a) watching the stars

b) growing plants

c) testing crystals

d) making new space foods

❷ Why is the ISS important to us?

a) It is a fun place to visit.

b) It gives us good pictures of Earth.

c) It helps us learn how to live in space.

d) It helps people learn to recycle.

D Mark T for true or F for false.

❶ The ISS has only one big computer. T F

❷ Most astronauts on the ISS speak English and Russian. T F

❸ Astronauts stay on the ISS for two days and then come back home. T F

❹ The ISS is 352 km above Earth. T F

Busy Morning in Space

An alarm rings.

The astronauts wake up.

They are in sleeping bags.

The sleeping bags are tied to the wall.

Everyone unzips their bags.

They stretch out their arms.

They float out of their bags.

Everything floats in the ISS.

Even astronauts float!

KEY WORDS

- busy
- alarm
- **ring** (ring-rang-rung)
- **wake up** (wake-woke-woken)
- sleeping bag
- **be tied to** (*cf.* tie)
- wall
- **unzip** (↔ zip)
- stretch out
- out of
- everything
- even

An astronaut washes his face.

Washing is different in space.

Water is stored in bags. **Aha!**

Some bags are big.

Some are for cooking.

Some are for experiments.

There are small bags of drinking water.

All the water is recycled.

The astronauts do not waste a drop!

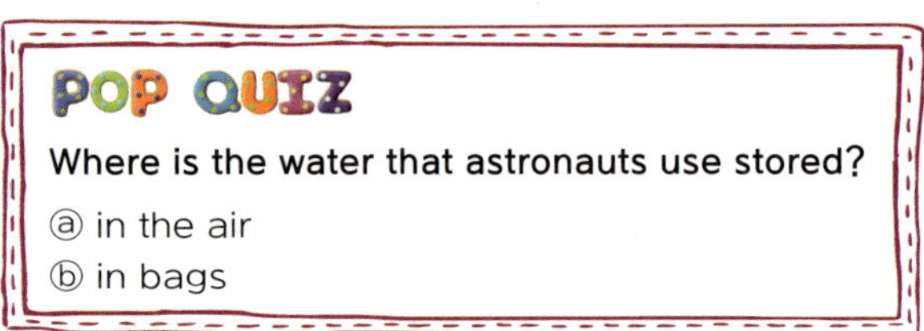

- wash one's face
  (*cf.* wash / washing)
- store
- cooking (*cf.* cook)
- drinking water (*cf.* drink)
- recycle

- waste
- drop
- pour
- get
- washcloth
- soap

- a bag of (*cf.* bag)
- put (put-put-put)
- a few
- then
- scrub

With no gravity, water does not pour.

Water floats.

The astronaut gets a washcloth.

He gets soap.

He gets a bag of water.

He puts a few drops on the washcloth.

Then he scrubs his face.

The astronaut brushes his teeth.

He gets a bag of water.

He puts a drop of water on his toothbrush.

He puts toothpaste on the brush.

He brushes his teeth.

He brushes up and down.

He brushes round and round.

Now he is done.

Where does the toothpaste go?

He spits it into a rag.

He takes a sip of water.

He wipes off his toothbrush.

He puts the rag in a bag.

He puts the bag in the trash.

KEY WORDS

- **brush one's teeth** (*cf.* brush / teeth)
- **toothbrush**
- **toothpaste**
- **up and down**
- **round and round**
- **done**

- **spit** (spit-spit/spat-spit/spat)
- **rag**
- **take a sip**
- **wipe off**
- **trash**

It is time to get dressed.

Today the astronaut puts on shorts.

He puts on a shirt.

He puts on socks.

Astronauts dress like you.

They have regular clothes.

They have pants.

They have shorts.

They have shirts.

They have socks.

They have tennis shoes.

They even have night clothes.

Astronauts have some special clothes, too.

They have launch suits.

They are for when a rocket takes off.

They have space suits.

They are for going outside of the ISS.

▲ launch suit

Astronauts cut each other's hair.

They have a vacuum hose.

The hose sucks up the hair.

▲ space suit

KEY WORDS

- special
- launch suit
- rocket
- take off
- space suit
- go outside (go-went-gone)(*cf.* outside)

- cut hair (cut-cut-cut)
- each other
- vacuum
- hose
- suck up

Now it is time to eat.

Off to the galley they go! **Aha!**

The galley is where they eat.

They push off the wall.

They push with their feet.

They pull with their hands.

They float in the ISS.

They float to the galley.

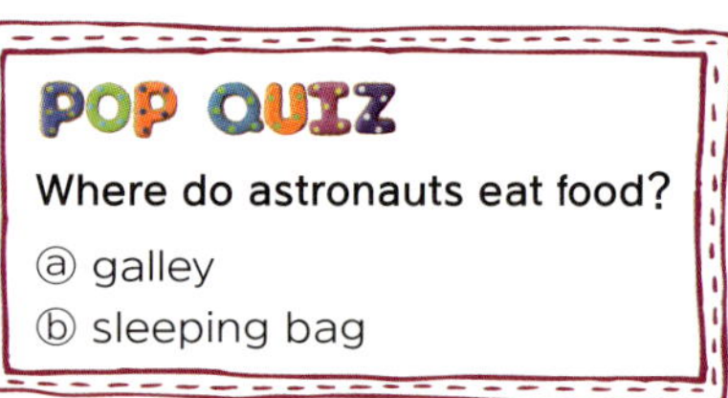

KEY WORDS

- **eat** (eat-ate-eaten)
- **go off**
- **galley**
- **push off**
- **feet**
- **pull**
- **breakfast drink** (*cf.* breakfast)
- **granola**
- **cool**
- **tea**
- **soft**
- **pouch**
- **tray**
- **lap**

Today they have a breakfast drink.

They have granola too.

They have cool tea.

All the food is in soft pouches.

They put the pouches on a tray.

One astronaut ties the tray to his lap.

Now he has a table on his lap!

Another astronaut ties his tray to a wall.

The trays hold the food pouches.

No one wants his food to float away.

The astronauts cut open the food pouches.

They put straws in the drink pouches.

Yum!

The food is good.

They are done eating breakfast.

They clean up.

They use wet wipes.

They wipe the spoons.

They wipe the trays.

They put everything away.

They all work together.

They keep the space station clean!

Chapter Two

Comprehension Quiz

A Mark T for true or F for false.

❶ Astronauts pour their drinks into cups. `T` `F`

❷ Astronauts use a vacuum hose when they cut their hair. `T` `F`

❸ Astronauts can wear regular clothes like you in the module. `T` `F`

❹ Trays can be used like a lap table. `T` `F`

B Choose the best answer to each question.

❶ How do astronauts move to the galley?

a) They take a bus.

b) They use the stairs.

c) They push and pull and float.

d) They run.

❷ Why do astronauts tie their sleeping bags to walls?

a) They don't need to put sleeping bags under the bed.

b) They don't need to roll them up.

c) They don't want get wet.

d) They don't want float away for sleeping.

C Solve the crossword puzzle.

❶ _________ means "of the sun."

❹ There is almost no _________ in space so things float.

❷ A drink pouch needs a _________ .

❸ All water in the ISS is _________ .

Astronauts Go to Work

After breakfast, the astronauts go to work.

They have much to do.

The astronauts check the gear.

They must be careful.

The ISS is full of gear.

They check things every day.

If something breaks, they fix it right away.

Checking takes a long time.

KEY WORDS

- go to work
- after
- have much to do
- check
- gear
- must + *Verb*

- careful
- be full of
- every day (*cf.* day)
- if
- something
- break (break-broke-broken)

- fix
- right away
- take + *Time*
- bin

The ISS is big.

There are many things to check.

Each thing has a place.

Some things are in boxes.

Some things are in bins.

Some things are tied to the wall.

Everything must be put away.

If not, it will float away.

Astronauts even check the equipment outside.

They do a spacewalk.

An astronaut puts on a space suit.

Space is very cold.

The space suit keeps him warm.

There is no air in space.

His space suit gives him air.

He needs tools to work.

His space suit has tools.

His space suit has a tether.

The tether ties him down.

He does not want to float away.

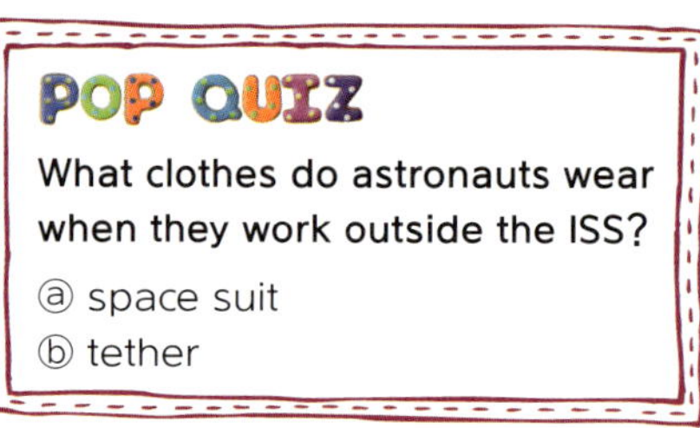

KEY WORDS

- equipment
- spacewalk
- cold
- warm
- air
- need
- tool
- tether
- tie ~ down

First, the astronaut goes into an airlock.

The airlock is a tiny room.

One door goes inside the ISS.

The other door goes outside to space.

He locks the door to the inside of the ISS.

This keeps the air inside.

Now he can open the door to space.

Then he leaves the airlock.

He goes outside.

He ties his suit to the ISS.

A strap on his suit has hooks.

It hooks onto the ISS.

The space suit has a light.

The sun sets every ninety minutes.

Then the sky is dark.

The astronaut turns on the light.

He checks the solar grid.

He checks the cameras.

He checks everything.

Astronauts use a special tool.

It is a robot arm.

The robot arm fixes things outside.

KEY WORDS

- first
- go into
- airlock
- tiny
- inside
- lock
- leave (leave-left-left)
- strap
- hook
- hook onto
- light
- set (set-set-set)
- ninety
- dark
- turn on (↔ turn off)
- robot arm

Now he goes back inside.

It is time to work out.

Astronauts work out every day.

It is important to stay strong. **Aha!**

In space, there is almost no gravity.

This makes people weak.

In space, people can move heavy things.

The things do not feel heavy.

Things seem light with no gravity.

Astronauts lift heavy weights.

They use a weight machine.

This keeps their bodies strong.

KEY WORDS

- **go back** (*cf.* back)
- **work out**
- **important**
- **stay**
- **strong**
- **weak**
- **heavy** (↔ light)
- **feel** (feel-felt-felt)
- **seem**
- **lift**
- **weight**
- **weight machine**

Astronauts run on the treadmill.

They put a heavy pack on their backs.

They tie a cord to their belts.

They tie the cord to the treadmill.

Then they run, run, run.

This keeps their hearts strong.

They also ride a bike.

It is an odd bike.

It does not have a seat.

The astronaut is tied
to it.

Their shoes are
snapped to it.

Then they ride, ride, ride!

Sometimes they like to play.

They do flips in the air.

They do turns.

They spin.

They act like acrobats.

KEY WORDS

- treadmill
- pack
- cord
- belt
- heart
- also

- ride (ride-rode-ridden)
- bike
- odd
- seat
- be snapped to (*cf.* snap)
- sometimes

- play
- flip
- turn
- spin (spin-spun-spun)
- act
- acrobat

Now it is time for a meeting. **Aha!**

It is the Daily Planning Meeting.

The astronauts call people on Earth.

Every day they talk to people on Earth.

They talk by video call.

They talk about the things they did.

They plan for the next day.

After the call, the astronauts talk.

They work as a team.

What do astronauts use when they have meetings with people on Earth?

ⓐ a cellular phone
ⓑ a video call

KEY WORDS

- it is time for
- daily
- planning meeting (*cf.* plan)
- talk
- by
- video call

The ISS has many cameras.

One is for NASA TV. Aha!

People ask the astronauts questions.

One question is, "What happens to water in space?"

The astronaut shows the people.

He puts water in his hand.

The water forms a ball.

He puts the ball of water on his head.

Then he lets it go.

The water floats in the air.

He opens his mouth.

He drinks the ball of water.

Some drops float away.

That is okay.

All water in the ISS is recycled.

- **NASA** (National Aeronautics and Space Administration)
- ask
- question
- happen to
- show
- form
- ball
- **let it go** (let-let-let)
- **okay** (= O.K., OK)

Here is another question.

"How do you wash your hair?"

One astronaut shows how.

She brushes her long hair.

It floats up.

She puts on no rinse shampoo.

She rubs her hair.

She dries it with a towel.

Then she brushes it again.

One person asks, "How do you train for space?"

Astronauts train at a space center.

They do things in a pool.

They train under the water.

It feels like space.

A boy asks, "How can I go to space?"

The astronaut tells him.

"Stay in school.

Study hard.

Be the best you can be.

Then you may get to go to NASA."

KEY WORDS

- wash one's hair
- no rinse (*cf.* rinse)
- rub
- dry
- towel
- train
- space center
- pool
- under the water
- hard
- best
- get to

Chapter Three

Comprehension Quiz

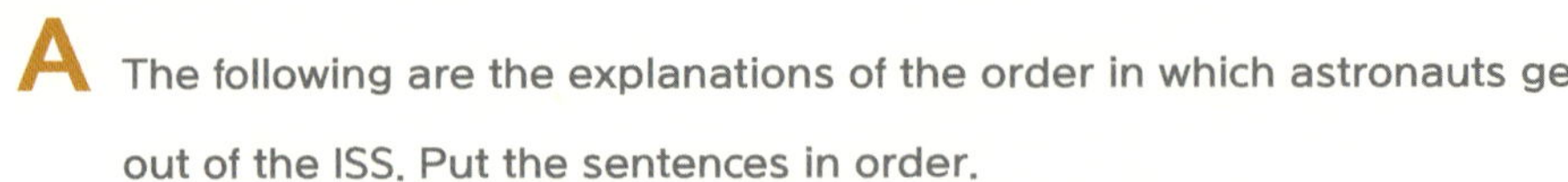

A The following are the explanations of the order in which astronauts get out of the ISS. Put the sentences in order.

❶ Go into the airlock.

❷ Lock the door to the inside of the ISS.

❸ Tie the space suit to the ISS.

❹ Open the door to space.

❺ Put on a space suit.

_______ → _______ → _______ → _______ → _______

B Mark T for true or F for false.

❶ Astronauts must work out every day.　　　　T F

❷ Astronauts wash their hair in a bathtub.　　　　T F

❸ Astronauts can use a robot arm to fix things.　　　　T F

❹ No gravity makes things feel heavy.　　　　T F

❶ Which one is NOT a function of space suits that astronauts put on to go outside the ISS?

a) keeping astronauts warm

b) giving astronauts air

c) tethering astronauts to the ISS

d) making astronauts float

❷ Which exercise do astronauts NOT do on the ISS?

a) swimming

b) running on a treadmill

c) riding a bike

d) lifting weights

❸ What do astronauts do through video calls with people on Earth?

a) Daily President's Visit

b) Daily Dinner Meeting

c) Daily Planning Meeting

d) Daily Workout

Astronauts Have Fun Too

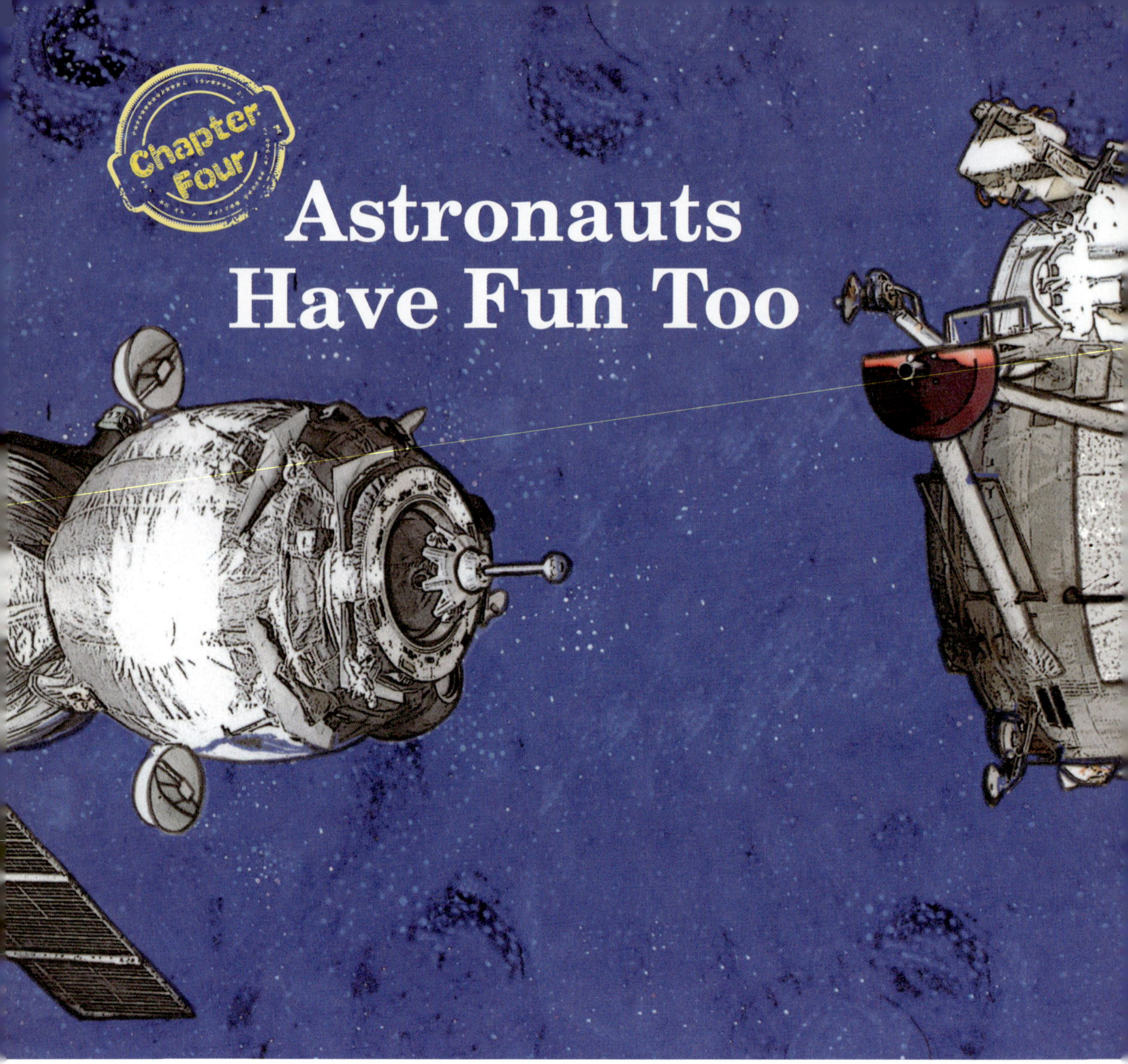

The astronauts are happy today.

They have a visitor.

It is a supply ship.

It is the Russian rocket Soyuz. 

The rocket ship docks.

An astronaut goes in the air lock.

This keeps the air in the ISS.

Then he opens the door to the rocket ship Soyuz.

He takes in many bags.

The astronauts help with the bags.

Some bags have space food.

Other bags have water.

Some have clothes.

One bag has fresh fruit.

This is a treat.

POP QUIZ

Mark T for true or F for false.

The Russian rocket ship Soyuz docks on the ISS to supply food, water and clothes.　　　T / F

Everyone goes to the galley.

They eat oranges.

They eat apples.

Then they eat dinner.

They may eat beef.

They may eat chicken.

They may eat green beans.

They have a special warmer.

It heats the food in the pouches.

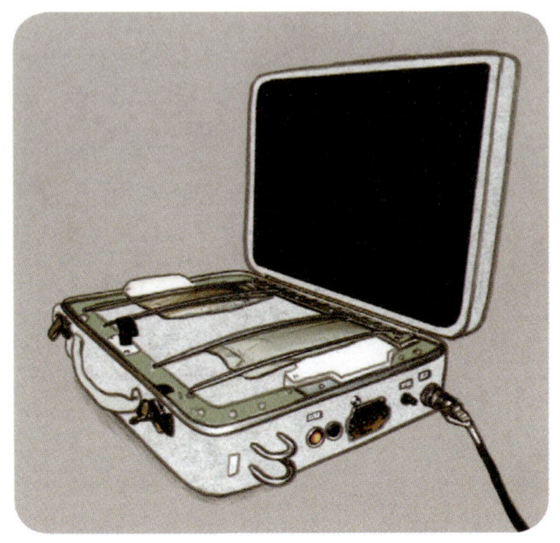

▲ a warmer which heats the food in the pouches

KEY WORDS

- dinner
- beef
- chicken
- green bean
- warmer
- heat
- dessert
- chocolate pudding (*cf.* pudding)
- taste

Now they eat dessert.

One astronaut eats chocolate pudding.

He puts a spoon in a pouch.

He lets the pudding float.

He is playing with his food!

Then he eats it.

After that, he drinks cool tea.

Space food tastes good.

Next, they check their email.

They get email every day.

They may call home, too.

They get a video call each week.

It is good to see family and friends.

- email
- get a call
- week

Now it is time to play.

"Do you want to play chess?" one of them asks. 

"Do you want to play basketball?" another one asks.

They decide to play both.

They play basketball.

They play with the ball in a big module.

▲ chess

POP QUIZ

Through what can astronauts see their family and friends on Earth?

ⓐ supply ship
ⓑ video call

▪ chess

▪ decide

▪ both

One astronaut throws the ball.

The ball floats.

The other astronaut hits it back.

One hits the ball with his knee. **Aha!**

Another hits it with his head.

They flip and turn.

KEY WORDS

- **throw** (throw-threw-thrown)
- **hit back** (hit-hit-hit)
- knee
- take out

- chessboard
- piece
- stick to
- magnet

- music
- soon
- dance
- love

Next, they take out a chessboard.

The chess pieces stick to the board.

They have magnets on them.

One astronaut turns on some music.

Soon everyone is dancing.

Everyone is spinning.

The astronauts love to dance.

Astronauts love to play!

Now they are tired.

It has been a long day.

It is almost time for bed.

An astronaut wants to take a bath.

But he cannot fill a bathtub.

The water will float away.

He wets a washcloth.

He puts soap on it.

He scrubs.

He washes his hair.

He dries off with a towel.

Now he is clean!

He brushes his teeth.

He puts on his night clothes.

He reads for a while.

He yawns.

KEY WORDS

- tired
- take a bath
- cannot (↔ can)

- fill
- bathtub
- dry off

- read (read-read-read)
- for a while
- yawn

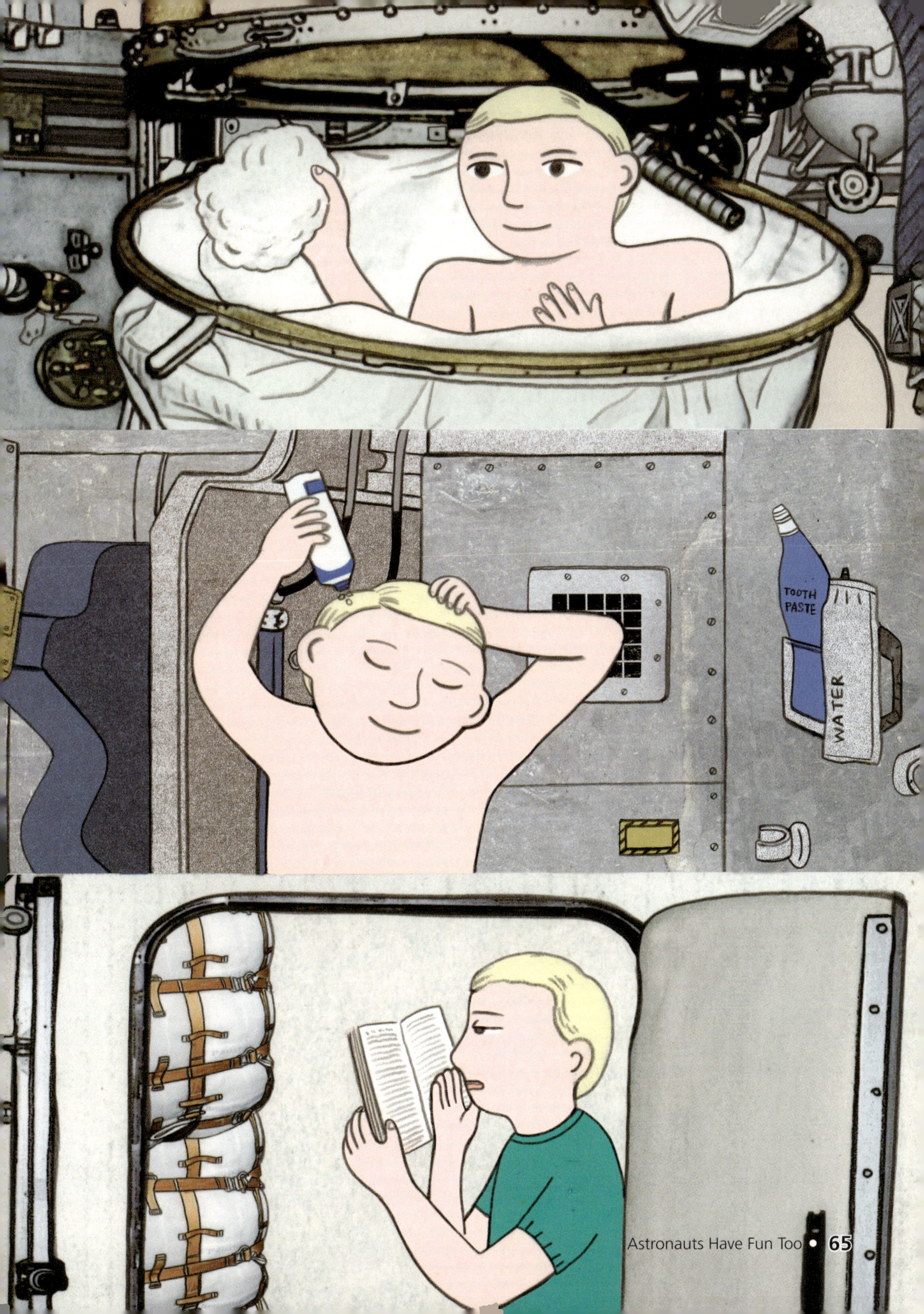

TOOTH PASTE
WATER

He gets into his sleeping bag.

He makes sure it is tied to the wall.

He does not want to float around.

He puts on a sleeping mask.

Then he goes to sleep.

Outside, the sun and stars shine.

They shine on the ISS.

Inside, the astronauts do not see the sunrises.

They are asleep. **Aha!**

In eight hours, they will start again.

It will be a new day on the ISS!

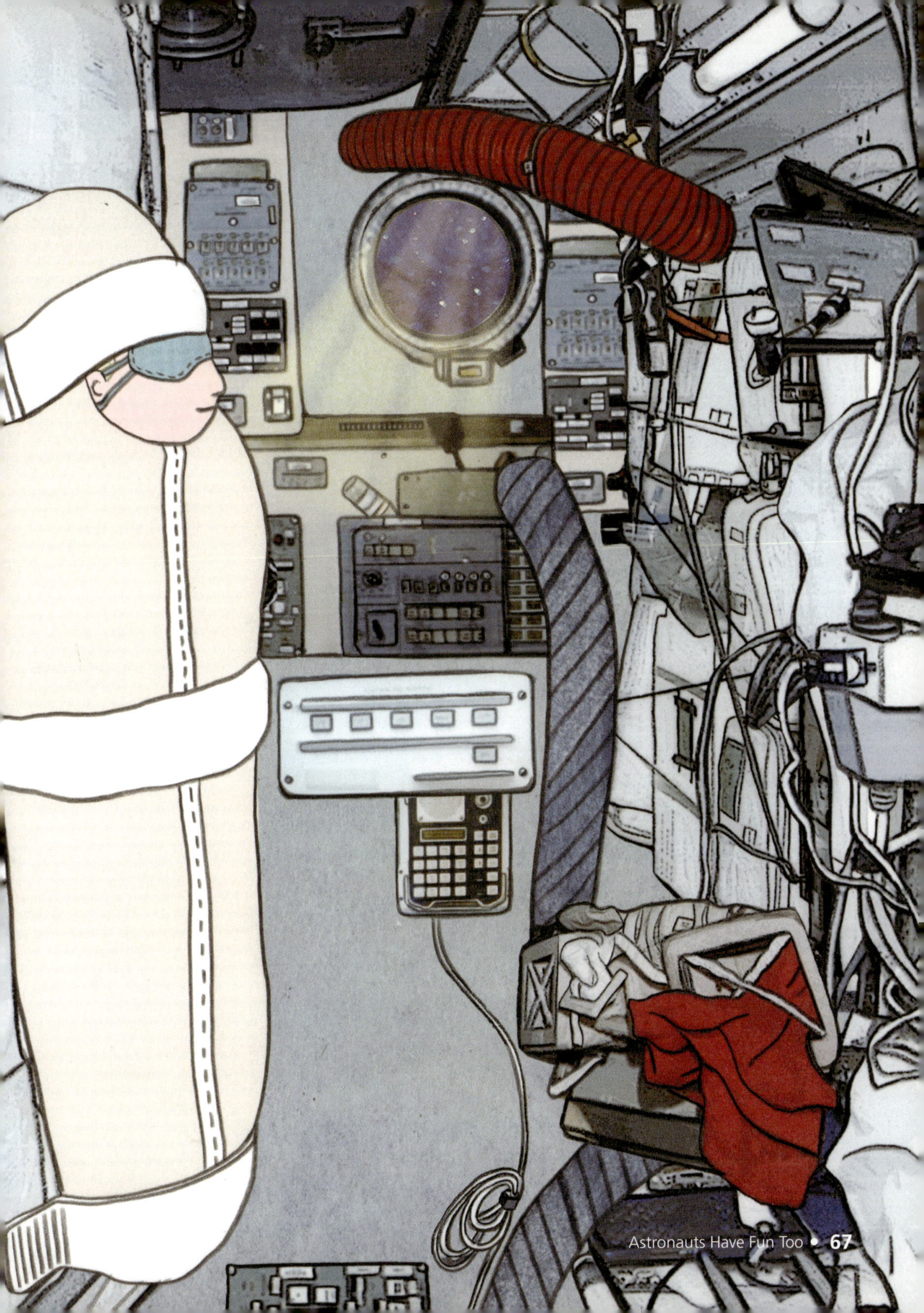

Comprehension Quiz

A Which one is NOT right about the rocket Soyuz?

a) It is the Russian rocket.

b) It is a supply ship.

c) It has many bags to give only water to ISS.

d) It docks on the ISS.

B Mark T for true or F for false.

❶ Astronauts eat some fruits. T F

❷ Astronauts never have visitors. T F

❸ Astronauts listen to music. T F

❹ Astronauts put on a sleeping mask when they go to sleep. T F

 Choose the best answer to each question.

❶ Which one is NOT a fun way that astronauts enjoy themselves on the ISS?

a) They play with their pets.

b) They play chess.

c) They play basketball.

d) They enjoy dancing.

❷ With what do astronauts heat their food?

a) regular oven

b) solar panel

c) special warmer

d) pot of boiling water

❸ Where do astronauts get fresh fruit?

a) from a garden on the ISS

b) from the grocery store

c) from the farmer's market

d) from the supply ship

Let's Review the Story

Fill in the blanks to review the story.

Title: A Day in S______

Place: The International Space Station

Chapter 1:
- The ISS is a base to e______ space.
- Astronauts do many science e______.
- Astronauts from many c______ live on the ISS.

Chapter 2:
- There is almost no g______ in space.
- Things f______ if they are not put away or tied down.
- Astronauts keep their food and water in p______.

Chapter 3:
- Astronauts w______ hard on the ISS.
- Astronauts work out every day to keep their bodies ______.

Chapter 4:
- Astronauts get email or a v______ call to see family and friends on Earth.
- Astronauts play games and listen to ______.

Let's Think & Talk

Think about the following questions and answer them freely.

❶ Among all the things astronauts do every day on the ISS, which one do you think is the most interesting? Which one would you want to experience in person? Tell us why you choose it.

❷ If you stayed on the ISS, which one would be the most difficult to do and why?

❸ Organize what you learned about the daily life of astronauts in space through the book.

Let's Review the Story

Title: A Day in Space

Place: The International Space Station

Chapter 1:

- The ISS is a base to explore space.
- Astronauts do many science experiments.
- Astronauts from many countries live on the ISS.

Chapter 2:

- There is almost no gravity in space.
- Things float if they are not put away or tied down.
- Astronauts keep their food and water in pouches.

Chapter 3:

- Astronauts work hard on the ISS.
- Astronauts work out every day to keep their bodies strong.

Chapter 4:

- Astronauts get email or a video call to see family and friends on Earth.
- Astronauts play games and listen to music.

Smart Readers: **Wise** & **Wide**

After-reading Test

- A Day in Space

- Level 1

- 18 Questions

  (Vocabulary 5 / Reading Comprehension 10 /

  Sentence Structure & Grammar 3)

1. Which of the following has a different meaning?

    ① tell   ② talk

    ③ speak   ④ work

2. Which of the following is similar to "get dressed"?

    ① put on   ② suck up

    ③ scrub   ④ go off

3. Which of the following is a pair of opposites?

    ① fresh ↔ special

    ② fly ↔ float

    ③ sunrise ↔ sunset

    ④ store ↔ recycle

4. Which pair has the wrong past tense form of the listed verb?

    ① grow − grew

    ② leave − left

    ③ go − went

    ④ hit − hitted

5. Choose the right word for the blank.

    > The ISS is full ___________ gear.

    ① with   ② off

    ③ of   ④ to

6. How long does it take the ISS to orbit Earth?
   ① 92 seconds   ② 92 minutes
   ③ 192 minutes   ④ 192 days

7. What do astronauts learn on the ISS?
   ① how to live in space
   ② how to play a musical instrument
   ③ how animals act in space
   ④ how to take pictures of Earth

8. What do astronauts NOT do after breakfast?
   ① checking the temperature of the water
   ② working out to keep their bodies strong
   ③ doing a spacewalk
   ④ checking the equipment and gear

9. Why do astronauts NOT fill the tub?
   ① There is not enough water.
   ② The water will float away.
   ③ It is too cold.
   ④ The tub is too small.

10. How different is chess in space from the game on Earth?
   ① The chess pieces have magnets on them.
   ② It doesn't need a chessboard.
   ③ It has balls instead of chess pieces.
   ④ It doesn't have a rule.

11. Where do astronauts take training to prepare to live in space?

    ① a pool at a space center

    ② underground at a space center

    ③ a supply ship at a space center

    ④ a tiny room at a space center

※ According to the story, choose the correct word(s) for the blank. (12~15)

12. ____________ is the room for eating meals.

    ① Airlock   ② NASA

    ③ Galley   ④ Sleeping bag

13. There is almost no ____________ in space.

    ① noise   ② gravity

    ③ waste   ④ star

14. Astronauts ____________ every drop of water in the ISS.

    ① recycle   ② drink

    ③ dock   ④ orbit

15. ____________ is worn when doing a spacewalk.

    ① Space suit   ② Launch suit

    ③ Night clothing   ④ Shorts

※ Choose the wrong part of the sentence. (16~17)

16.
There is more than 200 experiments!
① ② ③ ④

17.
In space, people can moving heavy things.
① ② ③ ④

18. What is the correct word for the blank?

The ISS helps us learn how to __________ along.

① get
② got
③ getting
④ gotten

Suzanne Pitner
Suzanne Pitner is a teacher and writer who has enjoyed visiting Alaska, exploring Rome, teaching in China, and is looking forward to more world travel. She has a Master's Degree in Education, and is a graduate of the Long Ridge Writer's Group. In addition to writing educational articles and books, she writes historical fiction and contemporary fiction for young adults using the pen name Suzanne Lilly.

Smart Readers
Wise & Wide 1-7

A Day in Space

Written by Suzanne Pitner
Illustrated by Juyoon Lee

First Published in September 2016

Editorial Manager: Juyon Choi
Editors: Jiyeong Park, Kyunghee Jang
Designers: Eunhee Lee, Elim
Cover Designer: Eunhee Lee

Published and distributed by

Happy House

Darakwon Bldg., 64-1 Jandari-ro, Mapo-gu, Seoul, Korea 04031
Tel: 82-2-736-2031(ext. 250)   Fax: 82-2-732-2037
Homepage: www.ihappyhouse.co.kr
Publisher: Kyudo Chung

ISBN: 978-89-6653-492-0 18740 / 978-89-6653-156-1 18740(set)

[Components]
• 1 Audio CD (Recording Studio: Aram)
• Answer Keys & Korean Translation: Free download at www.ihappyhouse.co.kr